THE

HISTORY OF PAPER MONEY

IN THE

PROVINCE OF MASSACHUSETTS BEFORE THE REVOLUTION,

WITH AN ACCOUNT OF

THE LAND BANK AND THE SILVER BANK.

Read before the American Statistical Association at Boston, May, 1874.

BY

E. H. DERBY.

THE NEW ENGLAND NEWS COMPANY,
Nos. 37 & 41, Court St., Boston, Mass.
1874.

THE

HISTORY OF PAPER MONEY

IN THE PROVINCE OF MASSACHUSETTS BEFORE THE REVOLUTION, WITH AN ACCOUNT OF THE LAND BANK AND THE SILVER BANK.

The colonists of Massachusetts, when they sought an asylum on the rugged coast of New England, took with them a very small supply of gold and silver. A few years after they landed, — as the elder Winthrop writes, — the scarcity of money was so great that their land and cattle fell to one-fourth of their previous value. The colonists sent most of their masts, fur, and fish to England to purchase supplies of tools and clothing, or to Virginia for corn; and, as these proved insufficient, their coin followed. They were soon obliged to resort to wampum, the Indian currency, and to constitute their peas, barley, and coin legal tenders at specific rates; and, although these were somewhat inconvenient for the ladies to use when they went a-shopping, they were easily divisible into small change.

When the vessels of the colonists reached the West Indies, they found there silver which had been circulated by the Spaniards or by the buccaneers; and, in 1652, had the courage to set up a mint, and coin a large number of pine-tree shillings. The tradition is, that the profits of the mint were so great that the mint-master paid as dower for his daughter, when she married, her weight in shillings; and that the maiden carried down the scale for a large amount of her father's coin.

But the home government soon interposed its veto. King Charles the Second complained that the royal prerogative was invaded. Thomas Temple, a friend of the colony, tried to convince him that the pine-tree on the shilling was the royal oak, but with indifferent success. The mint was soon interdicted, if not stopped; and the colony, restricted in its foreign trade, forbidden to manufacture, and exhausted by its long struggle with France, found its currency deficient.

Soon after the failure of an expedition to Quebec, in 1690, which cost it £50,000, it made its first emission of paper money, to the amount of £40,000, in bills of credit. At first, they were not favorably received; and the inscription upon them of "Honi soit qui mal y pense" seems to deprecate censure. These bills were signed by a committee composed of Penn Townsend, Adam Winthrop, and Timothy Thornton. To smooth their way, it was provided that their amount should not exceed four-fifths of the cost of the expedition; that they should be receivable for all taxes and duties, should be paid within a year, and be received by the Treasury at an advance of five per cent. The bills were duly redeemed, and some parties made profits from the premiums by repeated payments into the provincial Treasury.

Annual issues were made; and for thirteen years, during which the above safeguards were observed, there was but slight depreciation. But the war with France continued, and apparent success encouraged the Province to risk a future loss for a present relief, and the original precautions were discontinued. During the interval between 1703 and 1711, the periods for payment were extended from one to six years; the issues were increased; public confidence was shaken; and the bills, although made legal tenders by the acts of the Province, began to depreciate, and complaint was made of the scarcity of money.

Various efforts for relief were made. A land bank was proposed, to furnish currency, and build a bridge across Charles River; but this was frowned down as a South-Sea bubble, or

John-Law scheme, and the Assembly authorized more bills of credit.

The Council, which had voted down the project, was ready to favor a loan; and a loan of £50,000, in notes of the Province at five per cent, renewable for thirty years, was sanctioned in 1714, and the amount was loaned to private citizens.

Governor Dudley, who had become unpopular from his opposition to the bank, was superseded by Gov. Shute.

One loan did not suffice to relieve the Province, or supply it with a circulating medium. Specie disappeared, and new complaints arose as to its scarcity; and, in 1717, a new loan of £100,000 was made to the citizens in bills of credit, secured by mortgages to trustees appointed by the Province, the rate of interest being five per cent.

Under the influence of increasing currency and deferred payments, the bills of credit continued to fall, and silver rose to six shillings in coin for twelve in paper.

Counterfeits also made their appearance, and large expenses were incurred by the Province for improved paper and engraving. Litigation increased, and the current opinion of the day was, that the country would be ruined unless members should be sent to the legislature who would vote for more emissions of paper money.

A plan of a land bank was again presented, but was opposed by the solid men of Boston. The Assembly then voted a new issue of £100,000, in bills to be loaned at five per cent to private citizens; but Gov. Shute refused his assent to this measure, and a compromise was at length effected, by which half that amount was issued in loans, in 1720, redeemable in six to ten years. Gov. Shute is now recalled, and replaced by Gov. Dummer, upon whose accession Judge Sewall informs us that "the weight of depreciation had become intolerable oppression."

About this time, Madam Knight made her memorable journey from Boston to New York, seated on a pillion behind the postrider. In her journal, she describes the manners of Rhode Island and Connecticut, and of the Indian tribes through which she passed. She also gives a vivid description of the way in which the country trade was conducted; the trader's first question to his customer being, "How do you pay?" — the price of a penknife varying from sixpence to a shilling, as the payment was made in specie, bills, by barter, or credit.

In 1726, James Taylor writes that the emissions of bills of credit for the preceding ten years have amounted to £397,000, of which more than half are still outstanding; while silver coin has risen from 133, in 1710, to 283.

The historian, Douglas, estimates the bills of credit outstanding in 1728 at £314,000. In the same year, Gov. Burnet succeeds Gov. Dummer, and announces to the Province his instructions to give his assent to no acts authorizing bills of credit, until they shall be approved in England.

The rage for bills of credit now pervades other colonies; and the Logan of that day — who seems less partial to paper money than his namesake in the senate of the United States — writes from Pennsylvania to England, that "popular frenzy will not stop until the credit of this Province is as bad as that of New England, where an ounce of silver is worth twenty shillings in paper." Depreciation keeps pace with the growth of the currency. Public confidence is gone; but the call is not for gold or silver, but for more paper money, as it is now at Washington. The paper dollar passes for one-third of its nominal value. The £300,000 represent but £100,000, and some of the bills are for a penny only.

With a view to the relief of the public, the assembly provided that the bills of credit shall be a legal tender for debts by simple contract only, and not for bonds under seal. They also repealed the act which allowed the premium of five per cent on payments into the Treasury of the Province. It is due to the British governors of the Province to say that, for more than half a century, they strenuously opposed the issue of bills of credit; and their opposition to them led to disaffection, and often to their recall, as letters were addressed to the Board of Trade and influential men in England, suggesting that they were not acceptable to the Province. In 1729, Gov. Burnet is recalled, and his successor, Gov. Belcher, arrives, and assumes the government. He is instructed to allow no issue of bills in excess of the amount required to meet the annual charges of government, then ranging from £30,000 to £40,000 a year; but more bills are wanted, and the Assembly sends repeated requests to the king to modify these instructions. The king constantly refuses; even reproves the Assembly for the favor it has shown to such pernicious measures. From 1729 to 1741, there is an incessant struggle between the governor and the Assembly. Silver is now at more than three for one; and, in 1731, he gives a reluctant assent to the issue of bills to the amount of £76,500, which are barely equivalent to the charges of the Province. Rhode Island now issues £100,000, which circulate in Massachusetts; and private individuals put their own notes in circulation, and thus swell the current.

In 1737, bills of a new tenor are issued, containing express promises for payment at the specific rate of six shillings and eight pence the ounce of coin. These are issued to meet the public charges, but soon fall to a large discount. In 1739, the legislature of Massachusetts, "in one of their lucid intervals," as it is termed by the historian, Douglas, admit, in an act to prohibit the circulation of the bills of other provinces, the serious errors into which they have fallen.

This act recites "that the emission of great quantities of bills of public credit, without provision for their redemption, has stripped us of our money, and brought them into contempt, to the great scandal of the government; that the Province has fixed their value and time of redemption in 1742; and, as this may be frustrated by the circulation of bills of other provinces without such security, the same is prohibited in this province."

In 1740, a new issue, equivalent to £5,330 in specie, was made, to cover the current expenses of the Province, and provision is made for its redemption in 1742, at the rate of four for one.

While others favor a further issue of paper, the historian, Hutchinson, comes forward, at this juncture, as the champion of a silver currency. He submits a proposition for a loan in England at four per cent, and the importation of the proceeds of the loan into the Province in specie. At this moment, fifty thousand pounds in specie would have absorbed the whole circulation of the Province. The measure of Hutchinson did not prove acceptable to the Assembly, but it was the precursor of another, which finally extinguished the paper money of the Province. Massachusetts can afford to pardon the devotion of this able man to England, when she takes into account the value of his history, and the service he rendered her by the restoration of her currency.

But bills of credit had not yet reached their lowest stage of degradation. It is true that provincial bills were now selling at twenty-five per cent; but plans were afloat presaging a still further decline.

Two new projects were started tending to depress them: a plan for a land bank, and another for a partnership, termed a silver bank.

THE LAND BANK.

This project originated with John Coleman, who, in 1740, with his associates, Robert Hale, John Choate, Samuel Adams, and three hundred and ninety-one associates, published the prospectus of a Land Bank, or Bank of Manufactures. This was organized without a charter, and set in motion against the opposition of the governor. Its very name was specious and alluring, as land was considered the most solid of securities, and a strong desire to build up manufactures pervaded the Province. The prospectus of this bank was, that each partner should subscribe for £100 to £2,000 of the stock, and pay in a fifth of one per cent on his subscription, and then borrow the residue of his subscription from the bank, at three per cent on a loan payable in twenty annual instalments, the amount to be received by him in the bills of the bank; and his notes were payable in the productions of the Province; viz., hemp, flax, wool, wax, cordage, iron, linen, leather, flaxseed, cloth, canvas, copper, tallow, and cord-wood, at prices to be fixed by the directors, or in bank bills of the bank, payable in fifteen years. The measure seemed to combine currency with long loans at low rates of interest, to encourage the farmers and manufacturers, and to give the debtor the advantage of paying in his produce or manufactures, or in bank bills, should they deteriorate. But the governor issued his proclamation against the measure as a delusive and fraudulent scheme. It came before the Council to obtain a charter, and was there defeated; and, after its defeat, its directors undertook to file its articles of association with the secretary of the Province. It was carried into politics, and obtained a majority of the Assembly; and the Assembly chose its directors members of the Council. The governor, however, had the courage to veto the new councillors, and to dismiss from office all magistrates and officers of the militia who took part in the organization or direction of the bank. He then appealed to Parliament for an act to prohibit all such institutions. His determined opposition, however, did not deter the directors from making loans or issuing bills receivable for all debts due to the bank, to the amount of £100,000.

THE SILVER BANK.

This was a private partnership, or association, composed of one hundred and six merchants of Boston and its vicinity. Among them we find many familiar names, such as Oxnard, Oliver, Sewall, Bowdoin, Winslow, and other men of note in the Province, while there were others of inferior repute and credit. The project was, to subscribe £150,000, to take notes payable in fifteen years, in silver, at the rate of twenty shillings per ounce of coin, — or three times its actual value, — and to issue bills for circulation payable in fifteen years, at the rate of six shillings in silver for twenty in bills. There is reason to believe that the great solicitude for these banks sprung from the fact that the Province had pledged itself to redeem its bills within three years, under acts of the legislature, and that some of the loans made by the Province were becoming payable. Both the Land Bank and the Silver Bank were opposed by the governor; and so great was the excitement upon this subject, that rumors were spread of an insurrection to compel the governor and council to give their sanction to the banks; and warrants were issued for the arrest of the ringleaders.

But Gov. Belcher was resolute and obdurate, and arrested the ringleaders. The managers of the banks, however, were able, by misrepresentations abroad, to undermine his power in London, and effect his removal. They were, however, less successful in establishing the banks he had done so much to defeat; for, in 1742, Parliament passed acts prohibiting the issue of bills of credit, bank-notes, or currency, in any of the provinces, by any association without a charter. The banks fell; and, for twenty years after their fall, the rash and adventurous men who had embarked in them were involved in wearisome litigation, while the bills they had issued carried down with them the bills of the Province.

The fall of the Land and Silver Banks stopped many similar projects in the counties of Essex, Plymouth, and Middlesex, and the adjacent provinces of Rhode Island and New Hampshire; but the depreciation still continued; and, in 1740, the Rev. William Cooper draws the attention of the governor, assembly, and people to "an empty treasury, a defenceless country, and an embarrassed trade."

Gov. Belcher, who, for ten years, while governor of the Province, so strenuously opposed the paper currency, which finally swept him away, was one of the most distinguished sons of Massachusetts. Born in Boston, he graduated at Harvard College, in 1699, at the early age of seventeen. Inheriting a large fortune from his father, the most opulent merchant of the Province, he travelled for six years in Europe. With a fine person, agreeable manners, and many accomplishments, he went much into society, and made the acquaintance of George the Second, who subsequently became king of England, and who conferred on him several appointments. After his arduous contest with the banks and the Assembly, and removal from office in consequence of misstatements in London, he regained the favor of the king, and was made governor of New Jersey, where he was, for fourteen years, a very popular officer, as well as the founder, of Princeton College. He gave to it his library, at his decease. Massachusetts owes to him a debt of gratitude which she might well requite by rearing to him the monument in the churchyard at Cambridge which his heirs failed to erect, because his fortune was expended in her service; and New Jersey owes to him not only her college, but also her escape from a vitiated currency.

One of the last acts of Gov. Belcher was the dissolution of the Assembly; and, in his message to them of June, 1741, he tells them, "The management of the elections made yesterday discovers to me so much of the intentions of your house to support the fraudulent and pernicious scheme commonly called the Land Bank, condemned at home by his Majesty and Parliament, that I judge it derogatory to the king's honor and service, and inconsistent with the peace and welfare of the people, that you sit longer in General Assembly. I have therefore directed Secretary Willard to declare this Court dissolved."

The banks had exasperated the governor, and subverted the government, and finally fell before the omnipotence of Parliament. They were the bitter fruits of a depreciating currency, and of loans to debtors who had never expected to pay.

The new governor, William Shirley, who, in 1741, superseded the long-tried and faithful Belcher, showed more deference to the wishes of the Province and the views of its Assembly. He had a large family to provide for, and was anxious to conciliate those upon whom he depended for his salary; but he was deeply impressed, upon his arrival, with the wretched condition of affairs. In his first address to the Assembly, he expressed the hope "that Parliament would soon terminate the miseries accumulated upon the Province by the depreciation of bills"; observing "that it was flooded with bills issued either by itself or the adjacent provinces; that Rhode Island alone had issued £440,000 in bills of credit, of which £350,000 were circulating in Massachusetts."

The acts of Parliament to suppress the banks, and prohibiting the issue of currency by firms or individuals, soon after arrived. A committee of the Assembly report that £90,000 in bank-bills are still in circulation; and the governor recommends the Assembly to invite the other provinces to appoint commissioners to provide for the extinction of the paper currency; but the other provinces, who are drawing away the substance of Massachusetts, repeatedly refuse to unite in a Commission. In 1742, when the time for redeeming the currency approaches, the governor conciliates the Assembly by obtaining from England a remission of the restrictions on the issue of bills, and the Assembly reward him by a liberal salary. The state of the Province does not, however, improve; for, in 1744, the Rev. James Allen speaks, in his Election Sermon, of the difficulties in which we are involved "by an unhappy medium, uncertain as the winds, and fluctuating like the waves of the sea, through the unrighteousness which the land mourneth." There were unhappy and uncertain mediums then, as there are to-day, alike delusive, and alike under the ban of the clergy.

All further danger from the banks, however, is averted, and they are referred to as things of the past. In the language of the day, —

" The Land Bank and the Silver schemes
Were all last winter's noisy themes."

Other events were now at hand to delay the extinction of the bills, and to carry them still lower in the scale of depreciation.

In 1745, Gov. Shirley planned an expedition to Louisburg, the great fortress of France on the coast of Cape Breton. Wm. Vaughan, of New Hampshire, heartily co-operated with him, and may, possibly, have suggested the idea. A force of three thousand militia from Massachusetts, with eleven hundred more from the contiguous provinces, embarked in a fleet of a hundred sail of fishermen, with but eighteen cannon, to surprise or besiege a fortress defended by two hundred cannon and mortars, with walls forty feet thick at the base, and thirty feet high, and surrounded by a fosse eighty feet wide. This successful enterprise, guided by Pepperell, and aided by a few ships under Warren, gave Shirley a great prestige in England, but involved the Province in large expenses, which were met by depreciating bills. By the assiduous efforts of Shirley, England was led to consider the question of indemnity to the Province for the cost of an expedition national in its character, and the most important of the war. At this period, the Province was in great distress. Its paper currency exceeded £2,000,000, and its bills had fallen to eleven in paper for one in silver; and the Assembly, so long infatuated, began to see its errors, and admitted, in 1746, that "we have been the means of bringing distress, if not ruin, on ourselves."

The reign of paper money had lasted for fifty-nine years. It began in 1690, became oppressive in 1713, and insupportable at the close of the first half of the century; and, during this portion of the youth and young manhood of the State, its great interests — ship-building, the fisheries, and navigation — had actually declined; while the progress of population had been reduced one-half, doubling but once in half a century. Immense wrong had been done to widows, orphans, and the clergy, and to all salaried officers. Provincial loans had not relieved the public, while they had ruined merchants. The unhappy medium which had led to such results was denounced alike by the press, the pulpit, and the Council-chamber. In the verses of the day, —

> "The country maids with sauce to market come,
> And take their loads of tattered money home."

And well might such verses be heard or read, when it took eleven bills for one penny each to do the service of a penny in coin.

Again, Thomas Hutchinson proposed that the whole indemnity should be applied to the extinction of the paper money, and that the Province should return to specie payments. The governor urged this plan upon the Assembly, and at length it passed an act pledging the Province to apply whatever funds it should receive for indemnity to the payment of its bills; and, after such payment, to return to specie.

The merchants of London urged upon the government of Great Britain the policy of holding back the money until the necessary acts were passed in the Province; and Gov. Shirley promised to urge upon Parliament the prohibition of paper money in all the provinces.

The necessary acts were passed by the Assembly, and sent out to England; and the indemnity arrived in Boston, in the shape of 653,000 ounces of Spanish silver coins, and thirty tons of the copper coins of England.

But there were still to be delays. A party long opposed to paper money — including Douglas, the historian, with other prominent men — urged that it was unsafe to make so great a change at once as to return from silver at eleven for one to silver at par by a single step; that we should resume gradually, and wait for concert of action by the other provinces; insisting that a sudden change would give a shock to business, and transfer the trade to other provinces. But it was urged, in reply, that "nil utile quod non honestum"; that honesty was the best policy.

The bills began to rise with the prospect of payment, and the rate of redemption was advanced ten per cent; viz., to an average of one in silver for ten in paper. Nearly all the bills were redeemed at once by commissioners, and the residue received in the same year for taxes, at their fixed value; and thus was the paper money of Massachusetts happily extinguished, after a trial of more than half a century in bills of various tenors, payable sometimes in merchandise, and sometimes in silver, at rates varying from six shillings to sixty shillings per ounce. And the refrain of the streets rose from plaintive verse to —

"And now, old tenor, fare you well!
No more such tattered rags we'll tell.
Now dollars pass, for they are free;
It is a year of jubilee."

It was, indeed, a year of happiness. There was, it is true, a momentary pause while the silver was counted out for the paper; but trade, instead of leaving the Province, at once revived, at the cost of the adjacent provinces, which had hoped to profit by the bold act of Massachusetts. It became known as "the hard-money colony." In the succeeding ten years, it sent out four expeditions to Nova Scotia, the northern Lakes, and Canada, each larger than the expedition to Cape Breton. In a single year, it had ten thousand men under arms, and accomplished this without once suspending specie payments; and so increased its wealth and strength, in the quarter of a century which preceded the Revolution, that it made greater advances than it had done in the previous half-century, and was able to take the lead in the great struggle of the Revolution.

If it was safe for this Province, in 1749, to resume, when depressed by war and by a currency which had fallen to eleven for one in silver; if resumption then restored prosperity, how can the risk be great for us to resume, when we have, within six months, seen gold at 107, and exchange on England, payable in gold, at seven per cent below par? And how can a citizen of this State, with his history open beside him, reconcile himself to a further and unnecessary depreciation?

With gold at the lowest point for the last ten years, we have not only seen its change in our favor, — exports exceeding imports, gold accumulating, silver coin returning to its former channels, — but we have also seen freights and navigation improving, ship-building at the height of prosperity, with wages rising, and our productions in demand abroad; and now, shall we listen to the syren songs of those who would wreck us again on the dangerous shoals of paper money?

With the Revolution came another tide of irredeemable paper money. Massachusetts yielded to the pressure. She could not control the action of the continent; and, in three years, she saw the paper money decline from par to less than one per cent. The cause of freedom was nearly lost, not by the lack of patriotism, or the faltering hearts of its defenders, but by the inefficiency and disastrous effects of paper money.

The thirteen colonies owed much to the fleets and armies of France, but more to the supplies and silver circulated by her troops than to her fleets and armies. The cost of the war was greatly increased by the depreciation of the bills then so freely issued. Massachusetts fought on until her currency became worthless, and her proportion of the debt incurred during the war was equal to the value of her property. She resumed specie payments as soon as the government was re-established, and zealously maintained them for another half-century; indeed, for three-fourths of a century, if we exclude the exceptional and disastrous year of 1837.

From 1814 to 1819, when New York and all the States south and west of New England suspended, Massachusetts maintained specie payments, and escaped the losses by depreciation that befell other States; and it was not until New York opened her coffers to pay gold, and her great arteries of commerce, to which nature had contributed so much, that she began to gain upon Boston; and, since the Southern outbreak, both Massachusetts and Boston have maintained their credit at the highest point, and borrowed upon the most favorable terms, by constantly paying the interest and principal of their debts in gold, and are grateful to President Grant for his resistance of all schemes for inflation.

In conclusion, let me recognize my obligations to the histories of Douglas, Hutchinson, Bancroft, and Barry, to the biographical dictionary of Elliot, and to the very valuable compilation of Dr. Felt, for aid in the preparation of this essay.

AMERICAN STATISTICAL ASSOCIATION.

A quarterly meeting of this society was held in this city yesterday afternoon, the first vice-president, J. Wingate Thornton, in the chair. The recording secretary being absent, John Ward Dean was chosen secretary *pro tem.*

E. H. Derby then read a very interesting and carefully-prepared paper, entitled, "The History of Paper Money in the Province of Massachusetts Bay," in which he traced the history of paper money in Massachusetts, from its first issue, in 1690, to the end of the royal authority, giving instructive accounts of the Land Bank, the Silver Bank, and other schemes of inflation, with their disastrous results. He closed with a brief notice of the continental currency in the time of the Revolution, and its several stages of depreciation.

At the close of the paper, on motion of Mr. Thornton, it was

Voted, That the thanks of the association be presented to Mr. Derby for his learned and timely history of paper-money issue in New England, drawn from history for our own instruction.

www.ingramcontent.com/pod-product-compliance
Lightning Source LLC
LaVergne TN
LVHW010833120826
845149LV00016B/1365
9781418189853